G000145001

THE SURREY HILLS

Mike Cope

First published in Great Britain in 2010

The author would like to thank *Country Walking* magazine for permission to use extracts from previously published routes.

British Library Cataloguing-in-Publication Data
A CIP record for this title is available from the British Library

ISBN 978 1 906887 95 7

PiXZ Books
Halsgrove House, Ryelands Industrial Estate,
Bagley Road, Wellington, Somerset TA21 9PZ
Tel: 01823 653777
Fax: 01823 216796
email: sales@halsgrove.com

An imprint of Halstar Ltd, part of the Halsgrove group of companies
Information on all Halsgrove titles is available at: www.halsgrove.com

Printed and bound in China by Toppan Leefung Printing Ltd

Contents

How to use this book

The Area:

The Surrey Hills was one of the first areas in England to be designated an Area of Outstanding National Beauty (AONB) in 1958. It stretches across a quarter of the county and includes the chalk slopes of the North Downs, which run from Farnham to Oxted, and the deeply-forested Greensand Hills.

The North Downs sweep into Surrey from the east and terminate at the end of the Hog's Back. They have a distinctive topography with a steep, south-facing scarp slope and a shallow, north-facing dip slope. The valleys of the Wey and Mole are important corridors through the North Downs and transport services have been taken through these natural cuttings.

The Pilgrim's Way is an ancient trackway that runs along the edge of the North Downs escarpment, and was reputedly used by medieval pilgrims journeying from Winchester to Becket's shrine in Canterbury. It was Hilaire Belloc who wrote the first authoritative account of the Pilgrim's Way, in his 1904 book: *The Old Road*. For the most part, the ancient trackway keeps to the lower southern slopes, away from the exposed ridge, and avoids the sticky Gault Clay found on the lower ground. A National Trail, running alongside 'The Old Road', was first proposed by the Ramblers Association, and in 1978, The North Downs Way was officially opened by the Archbishop of Canterbury.

The Greensand Hills run roughly parallel to the North Downs, but further south, on the Lower Greensand ridge.

These prominent pine-forested hills are sometimes referred to as the 'Surrey Alps'. The underlying sandstone rocks, contain an uneven distribution of the mineral glauconite, giving them a greenish tinge. A pilot stretch of the Greensand Way was officially opened in 1980, and the whole 55 mile Surrey stretch from Haslemere to Limpsfield Chart was completed during the next two years.

Much of the North Downs is owned and managed by the National Trust. But certain areas (such as Newlands Corner and St Martha's Hill) are privately owned and public access is managed by Surrey Wildlife Trust under an access agreement with Surrey County Council. Ownership and management of the Greensand Hills are also divided. The National Trust owns Leith Hill, but Holmbury and Pitch Hill are privately owned and managed by the Hurtwood Control Trust.

The Routes:

Although the Surrey Hills AONB incorporates hills, woodlands, and heathland in its geographical catchment area, this book uses the word 'hills' in a more traditional sense. Seven of the routes are along the North Downs Way between Compton and Reigate and the remaining three are at prominent locations along the Greensand ridge, including Leith Hill, the highest point in south-east England.

All the routes are either circular or a figure of eight design. They range from 3 ¾ - 7 ½ miles and are graded from one to three boots – from easy to the more challenging.

Standard grid references are given for accurate location of starting points using an OS map (or mapping web-sites, such as www.multimap.com). A postcode or 'nearest postcode' is also given to locate the starting point with the aid of an in-car Sat Nav system. If the starting point is not near a postal address, then the 'nearest postcode' may be some distance away from the actual starting point.

The Maps

Although a thorough description of each walk is given and a sketch map provided, it is advisable to take with you a compass (or Sat Nav) and a detailed OS map of the area, should you stray from the route or are forced to cut it short. Conveniently, the whole area is covered by the 145 and 146 OS Explorer maps.

Key to Symbols Used

Level of difficulty:

Easy 🌸

Fair 🌸🌸

More challenging 🌸🌸🌸

Map symbols:

- Park & start
- Tarred Road
- Footpath
- Building / Town
- Pub
- Refreshments
- Triangulation pillar or other landmark
- Church
- WC

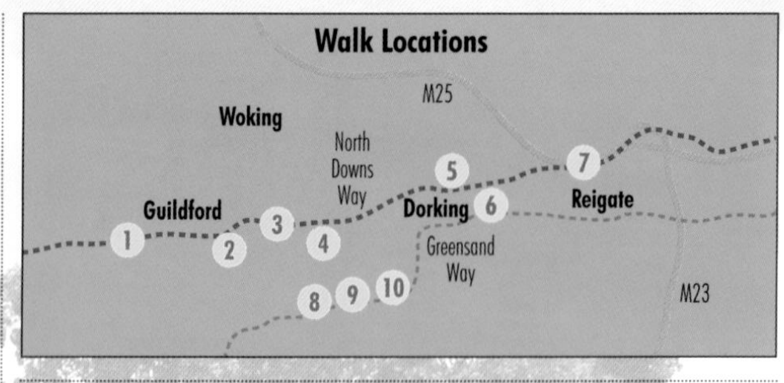

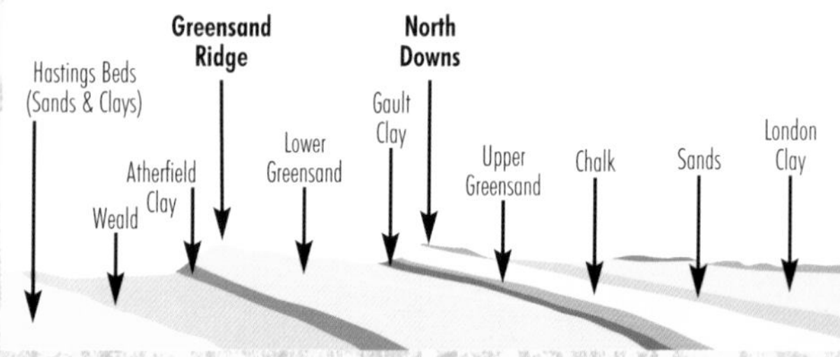

1 Compton and Guildford

A 6 ¾ mile inspirational circuit taking in an art gallery, a ruined chapel and a cathedral

Level:
Length: 6 ¾ miles (10.8Km)
Terrain: Undulating tracks around the North Downs Way; flat walking along the River Wey Navigation; steep final ascent near the end of the walk.
Park and start: The Mount, Guildford
Start ref: SU 985488
Postcode (nearest): GU2 4EY
Public transport: None to start, but Guildford railway station is walking distance from point 9
Refreshments and facilities:
Watts Gallery Tea Shop ; The Withies, Compton; Guildford pubs

Nestling at the foot of the North Downs, on its southern scarp slope, lies Compton and the Watts Gallery. Established in 1904, it contains an engaging collection of George Frederic Watts' work, from towering statues to pre-Raphaelite paintings. In his own life-time, Watts was widely considered to be the greatest painter of the Victorian age, enjoying an unparalleled reputation. The door to the lower galleries is embossed with the motto: 'The Utmost for the Highest'. His second wife, Mary, designed the cemetery chapel – an extraordinary, art nouveau, terracotta building, shaped like a Celtic cross - and the cloister where they're now buried. An even more famous grave lies en route: that of the Rev. Charles Lutwidge Dodgson (alias Lewis Carroll), the author of *Alice in Wonderland.*

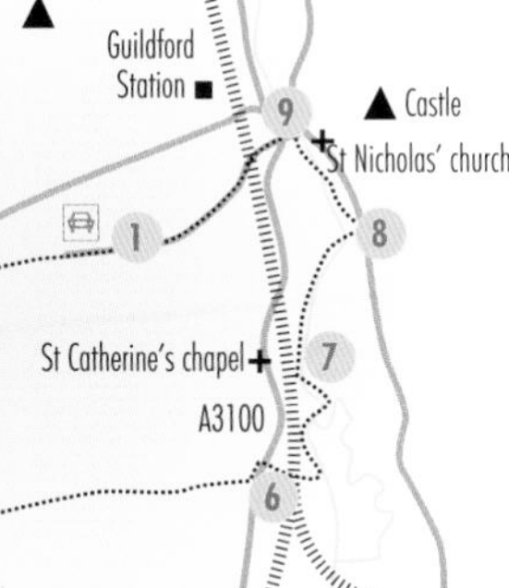

The Watts Gallery, Compton

1 Proceed uphill along the lane, passing a metal barrier and keep walking for 1km along a tree-lined track. After passing four large transmission masts, take the next left at the public footpath fingerpost. Cross a stile and proceed downhill towards farm buildings.

2 At the T-junction, bear right along the North Downs Way. Note the chalk pit on the hillside to your right and continue along a sandy track and through a wooded section. Go straight across at the next junction, past farm buildings. When you reach a road bear right to visit the Watts Gallery and teashop (recommended); to continue the walk, turn left along the road.

3 After 100 metres, go left at the public footpath fingerpost. If you wish to visit the Watts cemetery chapel, keep ahead along the road for another 400 metres, and return to this point to continue the walk. Proceed along the footpath that skirts the edge of woodland, and over a stile. At the next stile, turn right and then left along a wide concrete driveway. Zig zag right and then left over a stile to follow a path across marshy ground to another stile. Proceed along a narrow path that eventually drops down to a lane.

4 Turn right here and then left (after 30 metres) along a track towards Loseley House. Pass a cottage and when you reach a wooden gate with a sign saying 'Private', go left along the public footpath. Go over a half stile and follow the path as it bends to the right. Cross two more stiles and proceed towards the lake.

Loseley ice cream was first produced over 30 years ago at Loseley Park Estate. The More-Molyneux family began producing cheese, yoghurt and cream in the late 1960s and ice cream in 1977. The brand was eventually sold to the food giant Booker in 1987.

Watts cemetery chapel

Mistletoe near Loseley House

5 Look right for good views of Loseley House. Cross a stile and walk along the edge of a lake to another stile, and across two fields towards houses. Climb another stile and when you reach a road, go straight across, along a lane. When the lane ends, keep ahead along a footpath which climbs steadily uphill. At the top, a green church spire is visible in the distance. Continue downhill, past Surrey Police sports pavilion and playing fields on the left. The path soon becomes a metalled lane.

6 Turn left at the main road and then right after 150 metres along a public footpath. Go through a tunnel under the railway and when you reach the Wey Navigation towpath, turn left for Guildford.

7 The river meanders round a sharp left hand bend and then veers right, past a steep golden sandbank and under the Old Ferry footbridge. To visit the ruins of St Catherine's chapel (recommended), take the next footpath left, and at the main road bear left at the sign for St Catherine's Hill. To continue the walk, keep ahead along the towpath.

8 Cross a green bridge and follow the path as it cuts across a recreational area. Rejoin the towpath at Guildford Boat House and when the path ends, go left over a lattice girder bridge. Bear right through a car park and along a road. Pass a sculpture of Alice and the White Rabbit (on the right) and turn left at St Nicholas' church.

Although St Catherine's chapel is reputed to have been used by medieval pilgrims travelling from Winchester to Canterbury, it is more likely to have been built as a convenient place of worship for those living some distance away from the parish church of St Nicholas.

St Catherine's chapel

9 Go straight across, at the main road, into The Mount and walk uphill for a strenuous 1km. Some relief may be had by a short detour into Guildford Cemetery (left), to visit the grave of Lewis Carroll. Magnificent views of Guildford Cathedral open up, across the valley, as you ascend the 'Hill Difficulty' back to the starting point.

Lewis Carroll, the author of Alice in Wonderland, *never actually lived in Guildford, but the house where his six unmarried sisters lived (The Chestnuts) was rented in his name. He lived and worked in Oxford as a mathematics lecturer, but made frequent trips to Guildford to visit his sisters.*

Guildford cathedral

2 Chilworth and St Martha's Hill

A 7 mile circuit that combines remnants of former gunpowder mills with a hilltop chapel

The gunpowder mills at Chilworth were one of the most important centres for gunpowder production in Britain during the early nineteenth century. Saltpetre, sulphur and charcoal were carefully blended together and granulated by mill wheels, powered by the waters of the Tilling Bourne stream. William Cobbett visited the place in 1822 and condemned the making of gunpowder as 'the most damnable inventions that ever sprang from the minds of man, under the influence of the devil'. His remarks went unheeded for the next hundred years, until the massive downturn in demand for explosives at the end of the First World War caused the factory to close in 1920. Ivy, ferns and moss have now reclaimed what's left of the production buildings and incorporating mills.

Level:

Length: 7 miles (11.4Km)

Terrain: Very varied terrain along field paths, riverbank, and woodland. Steep, precarious descent from St Martha's Hill, towards end of walk.

Park and start: The Percy Arms pub car park (patrons only)

Start ref: TQ 030473

Postcode: GU4 8NP

Public transport: Chilworth station is right opposite the Percy Arms pub. Arriva buses 21 and 32 from Guildford to Redhill pass through Chilworth

Refreshments and facilities: The Percy Arms, Chilworth; The Seahorse pub, Shalford

Disused farm buildings

1 From the car park of the Percy Arms, proceed along the road past the Infant school and take the first footpath on the right, marked 'Vera's Path'. Cross a footbridge over the Tilling Bourne stream and then bear left along a tree-lined path. Pass a sequestered lake and remnants of former gunpowder works. When you reach green metal gates, go right along a road.

2 At the next bend, go half left at a fingerpost on rising ground. In due course, St Martha's Hill rises majestically from the meadow on your right hand side. Go left at the road and then through a gate into a large field. Follow the undulating field path, with wide uncluttered skies all around. Pass a disused farm building, and then proceed uphill through a cutting. Just beyond a large oak, take the next fingerpost on the left across a field. Descend a flight of steps to reach a lane, then turn right.

Field of yellow rapeseed

Shalford Mill

3 After a dwelling, take a footpath on the left that runs parallel to the road. Cross a stile and keep going along the hedgerow in the direction of the green spire. Cross another stile and then bear half left across a meadow. Climb another stile and cross a footbridge opposite Shalford Mill.

The River Wey Navigation was opened in 1653, and used to carry corn, flour, timber, and agricultural products from Guildford to London, and coal on the return journey. One of the first waterways to employ locks, it pre-dates the canal age by over a 100 years.

River Wey Navigation

4 Cross the road and go right, past the Seahorse pub at Shalford. Take the next left along a bridleway and follow the path as it bends left along a cycle way, towards Godalming. When you reach a railway bridge, near a mobile home park, maintain direction to pass houses on the right. Go half right at the next fork and follow a path to a road. Go right here and continue to a bridge.

5 Bear right along the River Wey Navigation towpath, pass under a railway bridge and continue past a lock. After a few river meanders, pass a steep bank of golden sand on left.

6 Bear immediately right over the river bridge (Old Ferry footbridge). Follow path (North Downs Way) through a marshy area and across parkland. When you reach a road, go straight across along Pilgrims Way. Continue uphill along road, and at the first left hand bend, fork right along the North Downs Way.

7 Keep ahead on this national trail for several miles, ignoring all turnoffs, with Chantry Wood on your right hand side.

8 When you eventually reach a road, zig zag left and then right. Keep going on this steadily ascending track until you reach St Martha's church.

9 After admiring the fabulous views, exit via the south gate of the churchyard to follow a sandy track with a metal fence on the right hand side. Continue down a steep and precarious path until you reach paddocks on the right hand side.

John Bunyan is reputed to have lived in Shalford and used the local geography for his Pilgrim's Progress. The 'Hill of Difficulty' may have been inspired by the long climb to St Martha's.

10 Go left at the next T-junction (ignoring sign to Chilworth village) along a narrow path. Cross the Tilling Bourne stream and just before you reach a second bridge, go right, past an information board. Proceed along river bank, past disused gunpowder works. Take the next left over a footbridge and retrace your steps to the car park of the Percy Arms pub.

St Martha's church

3 Albury and Shere

A legendary pool, an ancient church and a picture postcard village are all on offer on this 5 ¾ mile figure-of-eight ramble

It is possible to experience one of the finest viewpoints in Surrey, without having to venture more than a few hundred metres from the car park. Perhaps that is why Newlands Corner is such a popular meeting point and always teeming with people. For those who wish to venture further from the maddening crowd, there is Silent Pool, at the foot of Albury Downs. The pool is noted for its translucency and for the legends that surround it.

The sombre colours of the surrounding yew and box trees add to the pool's unearthly atmosphere. In 1926, a young women sparked off a police search when her car was found abandoned in a chalk pit near Newlands Corner. A few days later she calmly booked into a Harrogate hotel under the assumed name of Teresa Neele. The young woman was the crime fiction writer, Agatha Christie and Teresa Neele was the name of her husband's mistress.

Level:
Length: 5 ¾ miles (9.3 Km)
Terrain: Easy walking along rutted tracks, hollow lanes and waymarked footpaths. One appreciable ascent up the North Downs.
Park and start: Newlands Corner car park
Start ref: TQ 043492
Postcode (nearest): GU4 8SE
Public transport: Buses 21, 22 and 32 run from Guildford to Dorking and stop near Silent Pool
Refreshments and facilities: Newlands Corner café; Pubs and teashops in Shere

1 Walk back towards the main road and turn right 20 metres before it, along a public byway that leads downhill. The track bends to the left and becomes increasingly rutted, where rainwater has cut deep channels into the chalk. Pass ragged

The Catholic Apostolic church was built by Henry Drummond, owner of Albury Park, in1840. It became the spiritual centre for a body of Christians, who believed that the Second Coming was imminent. When the last minister died, the church closed its doors to the public for the very last time.

The Catholic Apostolic church in Albury

juniper bushes on the bank to your left, and when you reach a junction with a Second World War pillbox, swing right down a deeply rutted ancient track way, worn down by rain-water. You soon reach a metal gate on the right and the chalk pit where Agatha Christie's car was found abandoned. Ignore the next turning to the right and keep walking as the lane becomes sunken with steep banks on both sides.

Old parish church of Albury

2 Take the next left up a lane (public bridleway) which soon passes houses on the right. Keep on this track and when you reach a house fork right and then cross a stile. After 100 metres, fork right again, off the main track, up a footpath that goes along the edge of a quarry. Cross over the quarry access road and continue through a plantation of oak saplings. Cross two more stiles and when you reach a wooden fence over a stream, pause a while. The church now visible with its unusual gothic spires is the Catholic Apostolic.

3 Cross the road and turn right along the footpath. Keep ahead at the first sharp right hand bend and take the next left along a private drive to Albury Park. At the

next junction, fork left to visit the old parish church of Albury (well worth visiting), or right to continue the walk.

4 Go right at the fingerpost on rising ground, and through a kissing gate into the woods. Keep on the steadily ascending sandy path, ignoring all turnoffs. The path descends, crosses a junction, and enters woodland. Pass the gnarled trunks of old chestnut trees, before reaching a gate near a dwelling.

5 Turn immediately left, through a kissing gate, and follow the Shere Millennium parish trail. Follow the wide enclosed path through parkland, with fabulous views of the North Downs straight ahead. At the valley bottom, go through a gate and then right through Vickys gate, keeping the Tilling Bourne stream to your left. Notice the wonderful clarity of the water as you follow the path towards Shere village. Keep going until you reach a road with houses on the right.

Shere has been called 'the prettiest village in Surrey' and it is easy to see why with its picture postcard looks, and a tea shop that attracts a constant stream of visitors. Popular with movie makers, the village featured in the 2006 film 'The Holiday'.

Kissing gate near Shere

6 Keep ahead if you wish to make a detour to Shere village. To continue the walk, go left over a footbridge next to a ford. Take the first left up a footpath (Foxes way) with a brick wall on the left hand side. Cross a tarred lane and then pass through a spinney. Go through a metal kissing gate and along the left hand edge of a field.

7 Go through a second kissing gate and into woodland and then through a third gate and across a field of shortly cropped turf. The Catholic Apostolic church is now dead ahead of you. Go through a fourth kissing gate and when you reach a road, turn right along a footpath that runs just inside the hedge.

Silent Pool

8 At the busy A25, carefully cross both carriageways, then turn left. Turn right just before Silent Pool car park towards Sherbourne Farm. Pass the farm and take the next right for Silent Pool. When you reach the pool, go round it in a counter clockwise direction. Cross over the

The crystal clear waters of Silent Pool come from a freshwater spring which has passed through the chalk hillside of the North Downs. This acts as a filter and adds minerals, which explains why the water is bluish green and of exceptional clarity.

footbridge at the top of the pool and turn right to climb the man-made staircase. At the top, go left and then right to join a path that climbs uphill with a fence on the left. Pass a Second World War pillbox on the right and then begin the serious assault on the North Downs. This is by far the most arduous part of the walk.

9 When you reach the cross-roads at the brow of the hill, go left along the North Downs Way. Keep right (300 metres further along) and stay on the North Downs Way for another 1.5km, until you emerge at the busy main road, just opposite Newlands Corner car park.

Newlands Corner

4 Gomshall and Abinger

A bracing 7 ¼ mile circuit along the North Downs ridge and back via a sheltered valley

The village of Gomshall is situated on low sandy hills to the south of the Downs. One glimpse of its former industrial heritage is Gomshall Mill (now a restaurant), which was once used for milling corn. From the North Downs above Gomshall, there are spectacular views over the Weald to the Greensand ridge, with remains of World War II pillboxes all along the route.

Literary highlights include a wood (Piney Copse) once owned by the novelist E.M. Forster, who spent twenty years of his adult life living with his mother in Abinger Hammer, and a monument erected to Bishop Samuel Wilberforce, third son of the abolitionist, William Wilberforce, who was killed in a riding accident on the Abinger Roughs, in 1873.

Level:
Length: 7 ¼ miles (11.7Km)
Terrain: Gradual ascent of the North Downs, and then easy walking along the ridge. The return journey is along a sheltered, low level track across the Abinger Roughs.
Park and start: Gomshall railway station
Start ref: TQ 089478
Postcode: GU5 9NX
Public transport: Trains from Guildford and Redhill to Gomshall station
Refreshments and facilities: The Wotton Hatch; Wotton; The Compasses, Gomshall

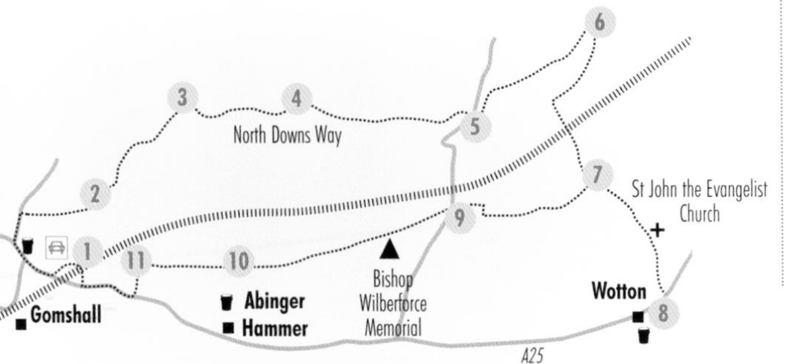

1 Go down the approach road to Gomshall station and turn right along the main road. Once past the Compasses pub, bear right up Colekitchen Lane, and take the first footpath right. Pass through two kissing gates and a wooded area, following the green waymarked path, which zigzags left and right.

2 Continue upwards through dense woodland, on a steadily climbing path. Pass through a gate before emerging into an open area. After a sign for Hackhurst Down, go through a gate and bear immediately left, through a kissing gate with the sign 'Sheep are grazing'. Ascend steeply, towards a chalk outcrop, with the remains of a World War II pillbox embedded in the hillside. Pause here for spectacular views across the Weald. Continue climbing and following the green self-guided trail, which bends to the left, before reaching a kissing gate.

3 Turn right here along the North Downs Way (NDW). Go straight over a public byway, through another kissing gate, and across an open area. At the T-junction, go right, along the NDW. Bear half left, at the next junction, to follow the yellow NDW waymarked trail.

4 Go through two more kissing gates, and keep ahead at the next footpath sign. Pass a number of World War II ('Dad's Army' constructed) pillboxes and then look out for an easily-missed chalk pit to the left of the track. At the next junction, bear right at the NDW sign.

Walking along the NDW above Abinger

In 1940 a network of defences was built all over England to repel an anticipated German invasion. Concrete pillboxes were sited all along the North Downs to form a 'stop line' to engage the advancing enemy before they reached London.

A World War II pillbox

Walking eastwards along the NDW

5 When you reach a road, zigzag right and then left across it, to follow the NDW. Not long afterwards, pass through a kissing gate, with dense woodland on the left and clear, unimpeded views to the right.

6 Go right at the next junction (before the pillbox), along a gradually descending track, lined with yew trees. Pause here for magnificant views over Dorking and the Greensand ridge. Ignore the first left turnoff, and follow the path though a kissing gate, along a field track and over a railway bridge, to a junction with a cluster of farm buildings.

7 Bear half left across a field, in the direction of the yellow waymark. Go through a kissing gate into woodland and cross a stile soon afterwards. Circumnavigate St John the Evangelist church and continue along the approach road to the Wotton Hatch pub.

St John the Evangelist church, Wotton

The Wotton Hatch pub was formerly called the Evelyn Arms, in honour of the Evelyn family, who lived nearby in Wotton house. Their famous son, John Evelyn, the 17th century diarist and contemporary of Samuel Pepys, is buried nearby in St John the Evangelist church, Wotton.

Bishop Samuel Wilberforce (aka 'Soapy Sam') is best remembered for a heated exchange between himself and the philosopher Thomas Huxley in the Oxford evolution debate in 1860, where he reputedly asked Huxley whether it was from his grandfather or grand-mother that he claimed descent from a monkey!

8 After a refreshing drink, retrace your steps to the junction near farm buildings. Bear left and follow the track between farm buildings. Pass a wood on the left and open fields on the right. Zig zag right and then left around a wood until you reach a road.

9 Cross it and follow the track into the Abinger Roughs. Keep ahead on this track ignoring all turnoffs. You will soon come to a monument dedicated to Bishop Samuel Wilberforce, who died here in a riding accident on 19 July 1873. Walk through woodland and across an open area. When you reach an intersection, take the middle fork, and immediately afterwards, fork right.

10 Keep ahead at the next junction, with spectacular views of the Downs to the right. Follow the blue way-mark through a kissing gate and on to a road. Zigzag right and immediately left along a path into National Trust land. Negotiate a kissing gate into Piney Copse, a wood once owned by the novel-ist E.M. Forster. The track gradually descends to a lane.

11 Bear left here and when you reach the main road, cross it, and continue right along the footpath. Re-cross the road before the bridge, when you see a blue sign for the station. Walk up the alley, and carefully cross the line to emerge at Gomshall station.

The novelist E.M. Forster, who wrote such classics as A Passage to India, A Room with a View, Howard's End *and* The Machine Stops, *spent twenty years of his adult life (1925-1945) living with his mother at West Hackhurst, Abinger Hammer.*

Bishop Wilberforce memorial

5 Box Hill and Mickleham

An exhilarating 7 mile walk around the Mole Valley from one of the most popular viewpoints in Southern England

North-east of Dorking, the North Downs rise spectacularly at Box Hill, one of the most popular viewpoints in Southern England. So called because of the ancient box trees on its flanks, it has been a popular picnic spot ever since the reign of Charles II, when John Evelyn, the diarist, praised its yew and box trees: 'it seeming from these evergreens to be summer all the winter'.

Prized for its close grain, box timber is so hard, that it can be carved precisely, making it ideal for engraving blocks. It is the heaviest English wood, and one famous engraver claimed that one of his blocks was sound after being used 900,000 times. Many of the box trees were cut down in the 18th century, when box was in high demand for engraving purposes.

Level:

Length: 7 miles (11.2 Km)

Terrain: Some steep and slippery descents around Box Hill and Mickleham; easy walking across vineyards, fields and woodland; gradual ascent over Juniper Top.

Park and start: Box Hill National Trust car park opposite the Shop and Information centre

Start ref: TQ 178514

Postcode: KT20 7LB

Public transport: Buses: Sunray travel 516 Leatherhead–Dorking;

Rail: Box Hill & West Humble station (½ mile); Dorking station (1mile)

Refreshments and facilities: Box Hill National Trust tea shop; Denbies Vineyard café; King William IV pub, Mickleham

Crossing the River Mole at the Stepping Stones

1 With the Box Hill National Trust Shop and Information Centre behind you, bear right along the road. After a sharp left hand bend, cross to the right hand side of the road and follow the gravel path to a concrete viewing platform with breath-taking views. Locate the trig point and then bear right along the North Downs Way. Follow the path downhill keeping to the North Downs Way, through a yew tree copse, and along a track reinforced with wooden planks. Proceed with caution as the track gets increasingly steeper. Soon you'll catch a glimpse of the River Mole below you, framed by dark yew and box trees. Continue downhill and cross the River Mole at the stepping stones. Go through the car park and cross the busy A24 dual carriageway.

Box Hill viewing platform

2 Pick up the North Downs Way again at the green gates and proceed down a lane and under a railway bridge. Go through a gate into Denbies

Wine Estate and keep ahead when you reach a four-way fingerpost. After this the track becomes increasingly steeper.

3 At the next junction, with a large laurel bush, bear right along a track that is fenced on both sides and soon becomes a metalled lane. Keep going until you reach the ruins of West Humble chapel and a road junction.

Denbies Wine Estate is the largest vineyard in England and has the same chalk soil structure as the famous champagne region of France. Around 400,000 bottles of wine are produced each year from over 300,000 vines.

4 Turn left here and then cut right after the West Humble 2000 AD signpost, across a field that climbs uphill. At the top, bear half left through woodland. Clamber over two stiles and at the road, bear right. When you reach Crabtree Lane car park, turn left into Norbury Park.

5 Follow the main bridleway for about 1km until you see a wooden fingerpost marked 'Viewpoint'. Enjoy the fine views across the Mole Valley to Box Hill and Mickleham church, then retrace your steps to the main track, and continue along the bridleway to pass Norbury Park sawmill on the left hand side.

West Humble Millennium signboard

6 Take the next right along a metalled lane that skirts the edge of Norbury Park estate. The road veers left and then downhill. Bear right at the wooden bench along a track that winds uphill. Keep ahead at the next two junctions and follow the track downhill past a mobile phone mast, and out of the woodland. Join a metalled lane, and when it veers sharp left, keep ahead along a bridleway. Bear right at the lane and cross the twin-arched bridge over the river Mole to meet the busy A24.

7 Turn left and follow the footpath along the dual carriageway. Cross with care, opposite the Frascati restaurant, and take the narrow lane to the King William IV pub, above it.

Viewpoint in Norbury Park

John Logie Baird, the inventor of the first working television set, lived at Swiss cottage, Box Hill from 1929-1932, and conducted some of his early experiments there, including the Noctovisor, an infra-red viewing device.

8 Turn right up the alleyway alongside the pub. At the top, bear half right along a track the climbs uphill. Take care as you navigate the next section of the walk. Keep climbing uphill, ignoring all turnoffs, until you reach a junction with a wooden post (marked 'Downs road'). Go right here and descend to a crossroads (with a green Box Hill information panel).

9 Bear left uphill along a narrow path. When the track veers sharp left at the summit, keep ahead past a yew tree. The path descends, swings right, and then continues past a bench and viewpoint. Eventually the track veers left and begins a steep and slippery descent to a road.

10 Go through Whitehill car park and bear left after 100 metres through a kissing gate. Keep to the obvious track for 1.5 Km and experience the wide open vistas of Juniper Top. Climb a stile into woodland and keep ahead at all crossroads. Go left at a T-junction and follow it to a road.

The King William IV pub, Mickleham

Denbies Vineyard from Box Hill

11 Turn right here and keep going until you reach the Box Hill NT car park.

John Keats stayed at the Burford Bridge Hotel, at the foot of Box Hill, and wrote his poem 'Endymion' there, in 1817. Jane Austen also visited Box Hill when she stayed with her cousin in Great Bookham, and used it for the setting of the picnic scene in her novel Emma.

Mickleham Millennium signboard

6 Brockham and Betchworth

A 7½ mile walk across a quintessentially English landscape, with inspiring views from the North Downs ridge

Brockham is the archetypal English village, with a church, two pubs and a shop, clustering around a village green. The River Mole meanders peacefully through it, and the dark green yews and disused chalk quarries of the North Downs grace its northern aspect.

But once a year the silence is broken, and thousands descend on this quiet Surrey village to witness a spectacular Guy Fawkes bonfire and fireworks display - one of the best in the region. But when the festivities are over, the revellers gone, and the rubbish cleared away, the tranquility returns and the village reverts back to its essential Englishness.

Level:

Length: 7½ miles (12Km)

Terrain: Easy walking across farmland; one gruelling ascent up scarp slope of North Downs; gentle scenic descent down to river valley.

Park and start: Christ Church, Brockham Green, Brockham

Start ref: TQ 198494

Postcode: RH3 7JR

Public transport: Number 32 Arriva bus goes from Guildford Friary bus station to Brockham Green via Dorking railway station

Refreshments and facilities: The Royal Oak and the Dukes Head, Brockham; The Dolphin, Betchworth; The Watermill, Dorking

Lych-gate of St Michael's

1 Walk across Brockham village green to the Dukes Head pub; bear right here, and then immediately left along a path that leads to a footbridge over the River Mole. Fork right and then right again at the next wooden signpost. Cross a wooden footbridge and follow the path across fields to a metal gate. Keep ahead through the churchyard of St Michael's Betchworth (used for filming 'Four Weddings and a Funeral') and exit via the northern lych-gate.

2 Proceed along the lane and turn left at the junction. Leave the road after 100 metres and continue along a path marked 'public footpath to school'. When you reach a road, go left and then immediately right up an alley by a post office. Swing right by an allotment area and follow the path as it meanders northwards.

3 Climb a stile and proceed to the busy A25. Cross with care and continue uphill across a field, bearing half left towards a phone mast. Cross a footbridge over the railway and continue uphill to woodland.

St Michael's, Betchworth

4 Cross a stile and then take the next right along a track that dips sharply downhill and then uphill again. Bear sharp left up a path with a wooden hand rail and then go right along the North Downs Way. Here is a good point to view the Brockham lime works and its disused kilns.The track dips down again through a gate and along an unmade road.

Chalk was once quarried at the Brockham Lime works, and a network of narrow gauge rail tracks carried it to lime kilns, where it was burnt to produce quicklime (calcium oxide). This was used in the building trade and for agricultural purposes.

Chalk outcrops north of Brockham

Chalk cliffs and autumn leaves

5 At the next junction, go left up a lane. At the top, bear half-left along a path, that climbs steeply uphill. Continue up this gru-elling, arduous ascent, along a path overgrown with buddleia. When you reach the top – sweaty and breathless – bear left; at the next junction, take the yellow waymarked track. Bear right at the wooden signpost, and then left at Box Hill road.

6 Continue for about 0.8km, passing caravan parks, then turn left along a public bridleway (opposite Headley Heath Approach).

7 Keep ahead at the wooden information board; the path now becomes rutted and descends rapidly through dark yew woodland.

Disused Lime Works

Bear sharp right at a wooden signpost up a steep staircase with wooden handrail. At the top take the left hand fork (with the purple waymark). Pass a bench with sensational views over Brockham, and the surrounding area. Continue down this gradually descending track for about 1.25km. At the end, go left along a downhill path that merges with a metalled lane.

The yew tree is native to Britain and thrives on chalky soil. The evergreen branches are so dense, that little can grow under them and the deep red timber is almost as durable as mahogany. Traditionally, long bows were made from imported yew.

8 Go under the railway and then bear immediately right, up steps and across a field. Cross another footbridge over the River Mole. At a signpost, bear left up a small track that brings you out on the busy A25. Cross it and turn left.

Brockham village green (in late October)

9 Take the next right along a road that leads to a golf club. Follow it round to the right and pass in front of the club house, and along the edge of the golf course. Cross the golf course, climb a stile, and walk towards a phone mast. Take the foot-bridge over the railway, and keep ahead until you reach a lane.

10 Go left and pass under the railway again. Keep on this track for about 0.7km. When you reach a stile near farm buildings, go left and then immediately right (at the next stile), along a lane. Turn left at the road and follow it round to your final destination – Brockham village.

Baled hay near Brockham

7 Reigate and Colley Hills

This short 3 ¾ mile route has breathtaking views along the line of the North Downs and across to the Greensand ridge

The view west from Colley Hill, along the spine of the North Downs, is truly breathtaking, with prominent quarries, standing out like white scars in the landscape. Leith Hill and the heavily wooded Greensand ridge form the southern aspect to this walk. En route, you will pass Reigate Fort, one of a number of mobilization centres that stretched across the North Downs, using the hills as a natural line of defence.

It was built in 1890 to protect London from foreign invasion at a time when confidence in the Naval forces was at a low ebb. The main threat was from the French, whose naval fleet was improving rapidly. The forts were originally designed as depots to supply troops with ammunition and equipment.

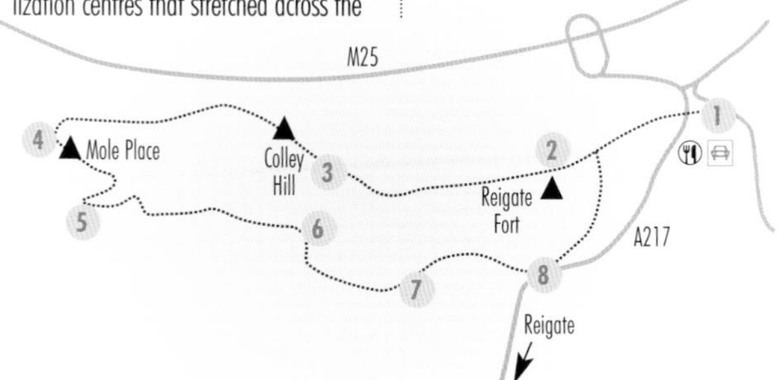

Level:

Length: 3 ¾ miles (6 Km)

Terrain: The route from Reigate to Colley Hill is family-friendly, and used by walkers, joggers and mountain bikers. Later on there are steep descents, that may be slippery in wet weather. The return leg is through woodland and urban fringe.

Park and start: Reigate Hill car park

Start ref: TQ 263523

Postcode(nearest): RH2 9RP

Public transport: None to start, but Arriva bus 32 goes from Guildford Friary bus station to Reigate via Dorking railway station

Refreshments and facilities: Reigate Hill refreshment hut

1 Locate the wooden refreshment hut on Reigate Hill and then turn right along the North Downs Way (NDW). Cross a footbridge over the main road and proceed along a wide track through beech woodland. Maintain direction at junction, when a metalled road merges from right, and pass houses on left.

Reigate Hill

Path from Reigate to Colley Hill

2 The entrance to Reigate Fort will soon appear on the left. Enter Fort for exhilarating views over Reigate and beyond. To continue the walk, keep ahead along NDW, past two mobile phone masts on right. This section of the NDW is a family-friendly track used by walkers, joggers and mountain bikers.

3 Pass through a gate to reach the white classical-style pavilion on Colley Hill presented by Inglis to the Borough of Reigate. Savour the jaw-dropping views on offer along the line of the North Downs to Box Hill and across to Leith Hill on the Greensand ridge; not to mention the jets taking off at Gatwick airport. This is an exceptional viewpoint and a fine example of rolling chalk downland. Continue along the gravel path of the NDW, as it veers away from the escarpment, and the downland gives way to shrub. Pass a disused water tower and then proceed through a gate. The path becomes increasingly enclosed with a wooden fence on the left and hedge on the right. Keep on main track, ignoring all turnoffs, and when you reach a metalled lane, go left.

Classical pavilion on Colley Hill

4 Pass Mole Place on right, and continue along an enclosed path that plunges steeply downhill through yew woodland. Their foliage is so dense that the ground beneath is virtually sterile. The sunken track resembles a bobsleigh run, as it banks sharply right and drops down to a 4-way junction.

5 Turn obliquely left along a public footpath (the Pilgrim's Way), with field on right hand side. Ignore stile on left and continue following yellow arrow. Pass an open area on left opposite a line of gnarled yews. Go down a flight of steps with a wooden handrail. Ignore path to right that follows line of wooden fence.

Flight of steps along the Pilgrim's Way

6 Branch immediately right at next fork, and continue along wooded path. Steep downland soon appears above you on the left. Keep following the yellow arrow, and take next fork left to join a wider track which merges from the right. Pass fields and horse paddocks on right and continue to a metalled lane.

7 Maintain direction and after a few hundred metres, fork left (blue arrow) along a bridleway to follow an enclosed path with a brick wall on the right. Soon the path becomes walled on both sides, with climbing plants trailing over the walls.

8 When you reach a busy main road, go left for 50 metres and then left again at the public footpath fingerpost. Take the path that leads uphill with green fencing on the left. Follow the yellow arrow, as path veers right and then begins a long, but gradual ascent up Reigate Hill. Near the top, a bridleway merges from the right. At the next junction (with small pond), go right and retrace your steps to Reigate Hill car park. The London skyline should be visible on a clear day from the field to your left.

View from Colley Hill

8 Peaslake and Pitch Hill

A 5 ¾ mile circular walk along forest tracks and pine woodland, encompassing one of the highest points on the Greensand ridge

Level:

Length: 5 ¾ miles (9.2Km)

Terrain: Gentle ascent to Pitch Hill and then easy walking along sandytracks and through pine woodland,

Park and start: Peaslake village car park behind the Hurtwood Inn

Start ref: TQ 086448

Postcode: GU5 9RR

Public transport: Arriva bus 25 from Guildford to Cranleigh stops in Peaslake.

Refreshments and facilities: Hurtwood Inn, Peaslake; Peaslake village stores

At the heart of the sleepy village of Peaslake stands the Hurtwood Inn, an atmospheric 1920's-style country inn, tastefully furnished to 3 star English Tourist Board quality and suitable for business breaks, romantic getaways, or mountain bike weekends. If you venture a few steps away from the Inn, you'll find yourself in an area known as the Hurtwood – the largest area of common land in Surrey, and one of the very first privately owned areas of the country to create a 'right to roam' in 1926. Since then the public have been given the right to walk and to ride, on horseback or mountain bike, over most of its 3000 acres in the heart of the Surrey hills. Two miles south of Peaslake on the Greensand ridge, you'll find Pitch Hill, which, at 257 metres, is the 5th highest point in Surrey.

The Hurtwood Inn signboard

1 With your back to the Hurtwood Inn, go right and then immediately left up a narrow metalled lane, to pass St Mark's church on the right. Keep on this steeply ascending track and when the lane ends, go half left through a wooden barrier to pass Peaslake cemetery, on the right. Keep on this broad sandy track through pine and oak woodland and when you reach a clearing with a cairn, fork right.

2 Continue along this steadily ascending track, and keep ahead at the next two junctions. The track eventually narrows and emerges from woodland. Pass a metal bench on the left hand side as another track merges from right soon after. Fork immediately left along path with a wooden handrail, with fabulous views of Holmbury and Leith Hill on the left.

3 At the pinnacle of Pitch Hill, go straight on towards the viewpoint and information board. To continue walk bear right to pass triangulation point and Hurtwood control collection box. Keep following the Greensand Way (GW) as it descends downhill through woodland, and take care to avoid tripping on exposed tree roots.

4 Before you reach Hurtwood control car park 3, bear left across a road, and follow the public footpath fingerpost in the direction of Mill Cottage. Squeeze through a narrow gap in the fence to follow the GW. Continue up a steep eroded path until you emerge in a clearing, with Ewhurst windmill (now a private

Peaslake village sign and pine cone logo

The view south from Pitch Hill

dwelling) on the left. Take the left fork along the GW, and maintain direction as the path descends through woodland. Ignore two crossing tracks and keep going until you reach a road. Keep ahead across road junction then turn left into Hurtwood control car park 4. Pass the information board and continue following the GW.

Ewhurst windmill stands on a promontory just north of Ewhurst village. It was built in 1845 and worked until 1885 with sails that rotated anticlockwise. In the 18th and 19th centuries the mill was reputedly a rendezvous for smugglers.

Ewhurst Windmill

The name Hurtwood may not derive – as is commonly thought – from the hurts, or bilberries that carpet the woodland floor, but may come from the Old English word 'churt' meaning a rough common, overrun with gorse, broom and bracken.

5 When you reach a bench and viewpoint at Reynard's Hill, keep following the GW as it veers to the right into birch and oak woodland. Branch right at the next fork and continue on main path until you see a tarmac road on the right. Gain the road at the first opportunity and bear left along it.

Mountain bikers near Reynard's Hill

6 When you reach a car parking area with a deep gulley behind it, bear right at the wooden fingerpost along a narrow sandy bridleway. Keep going along a path flanked with birch trees and bilberry bushes and branch right at the next fork. Pass a junction partially enclosed by wooden fences and keep ahead until you reach a complex junction of tracks. Maintain direction across junction and keep following the blue waymarked bridleway, with a small stream on the right and pine trees the size of telegraph poles on the left.

7 Cross a metalled lane and keep following the blue waymarked arrow, past three small ponds, along a slowly descending track. Pass under power lines and keep ahead at

Just beyond Hurtwood control car park 4

next junction. A wider track path merges from the right and then bends to the left. Keep going along the wide track, ignoring the next fork to the right. Pass a dwelling and then turn right, soon afterwards, along a sunken metalled lane.

Peaslake is a focal point for mountain biking in the area and the village stores is a popular re-fuelling stop for mountain bikers returning from rides in the nearby hills.

Deep gulley near Reynard's Hill

8 Bear right after 150 metres though Lockhurst Hatch Farm. Go through farm gate and then proceed along a narrow overgrown path. The path enters woodland and then widens out slightly. Go left at next T-junction and then branch right at the next fork along a blue waymarked bridleway. Follow this narrow path past a large country house, until it becomes a metalled lane.

9 When you reach a road, go left and then right approx. 100 metres later, along a blue waymarked bridleway (N.B. this is not the wide farm track, but the smaller path to the left of it). Look left for fabulous views of the North Downs above Shere. Keep going along the field edge, though a gate and up a small rise. Go though a field gate and bear left when you reach a road. After approx.100 metres there is a triangular road sign with a deer on it, next to a wooden barn.

10 Go right here along a field path, until you reach a narrow alleyway with a metal handrail. Keep on this steeply descending path, which brings you out opposite the Hurtwood Inn, Peaslake.

9 Holmbury Hill

A 5 ½ mile hike through the rugged pine-forested hills of the 'Surrey Alps'

The views from Holmbury Hill (261m) are some of the finest in Surrey. On a clear day, you can see over 20 miles across the Weald to Chanctonbury Ring, the Shoreham Gap and the English Channel. The views to the west are equally impressive – Hascombe Hill, the Devil's Punchbowl and Black Down. The remains of a hill fort, thought to have been built by an Iron Age community between 150 and 50 BC, crowns the summit of Holmbury Hill.

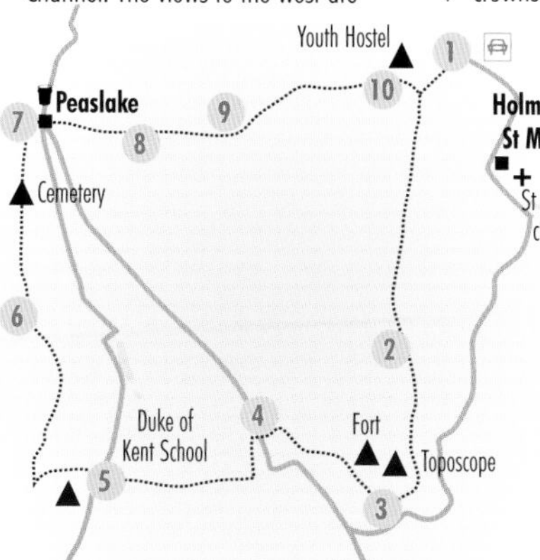

Down through the centuries the fort area has been used as a beacon station for warning and celebration – a reminder of the importance of this hill top location in bygone days. The settlements in the valleys, Peaslake and Holmbury St Mary, have something of the character of mountain villages, with a distinct feeling of remoteness.

Level:
Length: 5 ½ miles (9 km)
Terrain: Moderate ascent of one of the highest points on the Greensand ridge. Easy walking along sandy tracks and through pine woodland.
Park and start: Hurtwood control car park no. 9 (Holmbury St Mary)
Start ref: TQ 108451
Postcode (nearest): RH5 6NL
Public transport: None to start; Arriva bus 25 (Guildford to Cranleigh) stops at the Peaslake memorial
Refreshments and facilities: The Hurtwood Inn, Peaslake; Peaslake village stores; The Royal Oak, Holmbury St Mary; The Volunteer, Abinger Hammer

1 From Hurtwood control car park no. 9, take the rising path between the gate and the information board. Keep ascending on this wide sandy bridleway for approx.1200 metres, until you reach a five ways junction with a green bench.

2 Keep ahead and take the next right fork (yellow waymark). Go through a wooden barrier and into woodland. The path veers left and drops down to a junction near a green 'Holmbury Hillfort' sign. Keep ahead and follow the undulating path in a clockwise direction, until you reach the summit of Holmbury Hill.

Near the summit of Holmbury Hill

The toposcope on Holmbury Hill

The toposcope on Holmbury Hill is an popular meeting point for mountain bikers and the starting point for the following trails, affectionately known as : Yoghurt pots (aka Parklife), Reservoir Dogs, Barry Knows Best and Telegraph Road.

3 Locate the trig point and go through gap, following the white Greensand Way (GW) arrow. At the next fork, go right and merge with a wider track. Follow this downhill until you reach a junction and a small pond. Go left through a car park and continue until you reach a road.

4 Cross it and branch immediately left. Go left at junction and then fork right at yellow GW sign. Follow the narrow enclosed footpath across open pasture and maintain direction until you reach a road.

Hammond's Pond

The bathing scene with Lucy Honeychurch in E.M. Forster's novel A Room with a View *(1908) is believed to be a pond on Holmbury Hill, and the village of Summer Street, Holmbury St Mary.*

Peaslake village stores

5 Go straight across through the grounds of the Duke of Kent School, keeping to the right of the access road and follow the white GW waymark up wooden steps into woodland. Locate a wooden railing on left and continue up a steep ascent and through a kissing gate. Turn right along a wide forest ride and follow it downhill. Maintain direction when another track merges from the left, near a triangular clearing.

Entrance to Duke of Kent School

6 Keep on the obvious path, ignoring next left fork, until you come to Peaslake cemetery. Go through wooden barrier and then bear half left to join a metalled lane, that drops down to Peaslake village.

7 Turn right at road, past Hurtwood Inn and right again at the village stores (stopping here to sample tea and home made cakes). Bear left up Radnor road and then immediately left up a steep bank (Shere parish millennium trail).Go straight across at wooden barrier and along metalled lane. Go through another barrier and along a wooded avenue.

8 Cross a junction and keep ahead when you reach a complex junction in a hollow. Proceed uphill along a dark, eroded path, keeping field to the left.

Ponds near Holmbury St Mary Youth Hostel

9 At the next complex junction (under a beech canopy), go half left. Cross next junction and follow the undulating path until you come to a wide walkway with two ponds on each side. Keep on the obvious path and take the next left fork, which leads you past Holmbury St Mary Youth Hostel.

10 Maintain direction along a path bordered by bilberries (hurts), which eventually drops down to a wide, sandy bridleway. Turn left and retrace your steps to the car park.

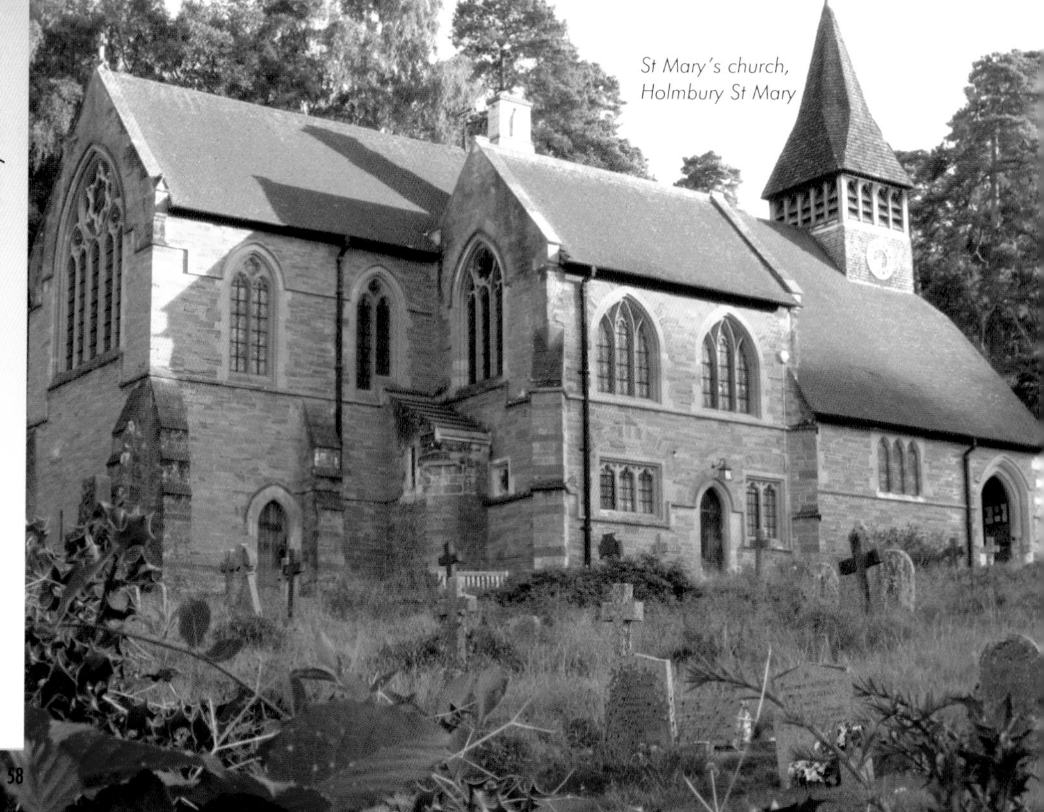

St Mary's church, Holmbury St Mary

10 Leith Hill and Friday Street

A 5 ¾ mile ramble from the highest point in South-East England to one of the smallest and remotest hamlets in Surrey

Level:

Length: 5 ¾ miles (9.2 Km)

Terrain: Easily walked woodland tracks with some moderate ascents towards end of walk

Park and start: Starveall Corner car park

Start ref: TQ 131432

Postcode(nearest): RH5 6LU

Public transport: None to start

Refreshments and facilities: The Stephan Langton pub, Friday Street; kiosk at Leith Hill tower sells cakes and hot drinks throughout the year (but check for opening times)

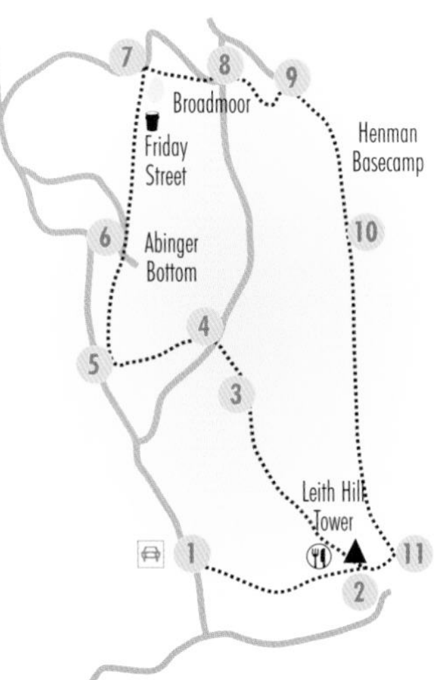

Leith Hill tower and folly was built in 1765 by Richard Hull, of Leith Hill Place, to raise the height of Leith Hill from 967 feet to above the 1000 foot mark. When Richard Hull died he was buried beneath the tower floor. In return for climbing the 75 spiral steps to the top of the battlements, there are panoramic views that stretch from inner London (St Paul's and the London Eye) across the Weald to the English Channel.

Former occupants of Leith Hill Place include Caroline Wedgwood, eldest sister of the famous naturalist Charles Darwin, and the composer Ralph Vaughan Williams (Caroline's grandson), who donated Leith Hill Place to the National Trust in 1944.

1 From the Starveall Corner car park, locate the fingerpost 'Footpath to tower' and follow the circuitous path to Leith Hill tower.

2 Just before reaching the tower, bear left along a footpath. At the first junction, fork right, and continue on a steadily descending path. Pass through an area of rhododendron bushes and birch trees. The path now broadens out into a track wide enough for motor vehicles. At the next junction, veer left near a tiny pine copse.

Pine woods near Leith Hill tower

A frequent visitor to Leith Hill was the famous naturalist, Charles Darwin, whose eldest sister once lived at Leith Hill Place. The composer, Ralph Vaughan Williams, (a relative of Darwin) also spent his childhood there.

3 Soon after, bear right at the T-junction, along a wide track. Continue descending, as a track merges from right. Bear half left at the next junction with wooden finger-post and continue to a road.

Leith Hill tower

Kissing gate at point 4

4 Go straight across road to enter pine and beech woodland, and follow the descending path to a wooden kissing gate. Cross a field and go through another kissing gate. Continue along enclosed path with a holly hedge on left and fields on the right. As the path descends, note the fencing on the left made from custom-built hurdles.

Hurdle-making has been going on around Leith Hill since the 1870s. The portable wooden frames or screens can be used as temporary fences. There are basically two types: gate hurdles (made from cleft poles) and wattle hurdles (basket-like and made from interwoven rods).

5 At the next waymarked junction, turn right along a track that winds through the beautiful woodlands of Abinger Bottom, and eventually becomes a lane.

6 After passing houses on the left, bear half right along an (easily missed) bridleway that runs parallel to a stream. Go through a barrier, to join a lane, which passes through the charming and secluded hamlet of Friday Street.

The Stephen Langton pub, Friday Street

7 After passing the Stephen Langton pub, bear right across the end of the millpond, a former hammer pond that powered the hammers of Surrey's 16th century iron industry. At the far side, turn half right along a footpath that leads uphill away from the pond. Continue steadily uphill and cross a metalled lane.

Stephen Langton, Friday Street's most famous son, is an enigmatic, shadowy figure. He was Archbishop of Canterbury from 1207 to 1228, and had a prominent role in the drafting of the Magna Carta at Runneymede.

Millpond at Friday Street

8 Keep ahead and cross another metalled lane. Fork right, soon afterwards, along a narrow (easily missed) path. This path descends gradually and then more steeply. At the wooden waymark with the yellow arrow, bear right and then left, soon afterwards, to join a lane. Go left along lane through Broadmoor - another secluded hamlet.

9 Take the first right, opposite the riding centre, along a wide bridleway (the Greensand Way). Continue along this track, wide enough for motor vehicles, past Henman Basecamp.

10 Fork right at the next junction in the direction of Warren Farm. Continue walking uphill for a kilometre or so. The ascent eventually becomes steeper and when you reach a junction, bear right at a sign for Leith Hill.

11 Negotiate an even steeper climb to reach Leith Hill tower. Retrace your steps to the Starveall Corner car park.

Winter sunset at Leith Hill